TO PUBLIC SCHOOL MARY LEE GAVE HER ART
TEACHING CHILDREN INSPIRED EACH IN PART.
THE WORLD AS HER PALETTE
IS HER GREATEST TALENT
AND AS A FRIEND SHE HAS OUR HEART.

MARY LEE LIVES IN TIDEWATER VIRGINIA WITH HER HUSBAND. SHE IS
STILL TEACHING AT HER CHURCH. THIS CHURCH HAS STAINED GLASS
WINDOWS SHE DESIGNED AND HELPED COMPLETE. IF YOU LOOK
CLOSELY AT HER ART, MANY TIMES YOU WILL SEE VARIOUS CREATURES
HIDDEN IN THE PICTURES.

MARILYN K. TAUGHT HEALTH AT PRIVATE SCHOOL.
A COACH AND A REF-SHE IS WAY TOO COOL!
VOLUNTEERING HER ABILITY
TO BOARDS NEEDING STABILITY
AND AS A FRIEND SHE IS REALLY A JEWEL

MARILYN K. LIVES IN NORTHEAST OHIO WITH HER HUSBAND, SON, AND TWO VERY LUCKY
GOLDEN RETRIEVERS. SHE IS INVOLVED IN HER COMMUNITY AND CHURCH.

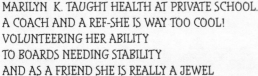

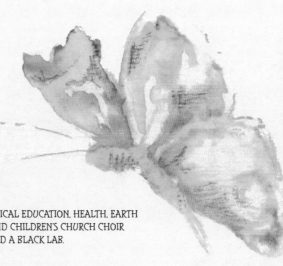

MARILYN A. TAUGHT WITH THE TWO OF GOLD
ALL WERE CAST FROM THE EXACT SAME MOLD
SHE'S THE VOLUNTEER QUEEN
FROM CHURCH TO THEATER SCENE
AND IS THE LINK FOR TRI-FRIENDSHIPS TAKING HOLD.

MARILYN A. LIVES IN CENTRAL KENTUCKY WITH HER HUSBAND. SHE TAUGHT PHYSICAL EDUCATION, HEALTH, EARTH
SCIENCE AND BIOLOGY. "MISS MARILYN" WAS THE PRESCHOOL MUSIC TEACHER AND CHILDREN'S CHURCH CHOIR
DIRECTOR FOR 25 YEARS. SHE HAS TWO RESCUED DOGS-A GOLDEN RETRIEVER AND A BLACK LAB.

ISBN: 1450553761
ISBN-13: 9781450553766

**DEDICATED
TO ALL GOD'S CREATURES**

Perpetually Preying Praying Mantis

The Life of Sue the Praying Mantis

By
Marilyn Anderson
Marilyn Kent

Illustrated by
Mary Lee Dunn

Look for the beauty in nature!
Marilyn Kent

Keep Praying
Marilyn Anderson

Artfully Dunn
Mary Lee Dunn

PRAYING MANTIS, A SPIRITUAL VISION
FOLDED FRONT PAWS, CAREFUL PRECISION

THEY TAKE THE STANCE
TO HAVE A CHANCE

AND PRAY FOR PREY, A NATURAL DECISION

ONCE WAS A MANTIS NAMED SUE
SHE WAS PRAYING FOR PREY IT IS TRUE

NOW CHOOSE YOU MUST
WHICH WAY YOU TRUST

SHOULD PREYING MANTIS BE THE TRUE CLUE?

THE EGG CASE ATTACHED TO THE WALL
WAS LAID BY MOM MANTIS THAT FALL

WHEN SPRINGTIME CAME NEAR
THREE HUNDRED BABIES APPEAR

WINGLESS COPIES, BUT OH, SO SMALL

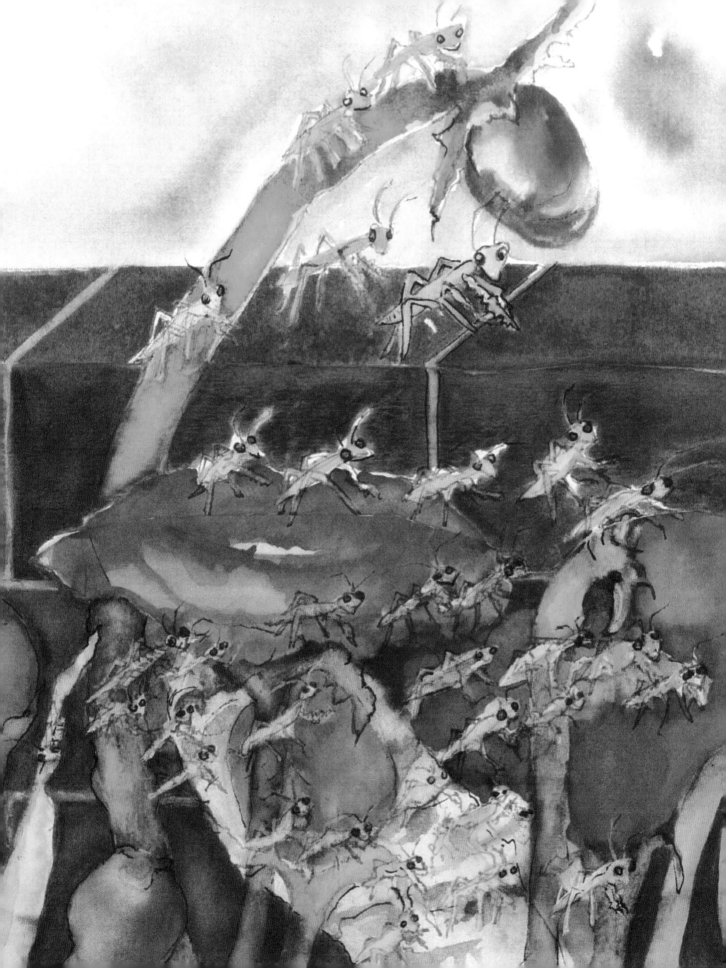

THERE ONCE WAS A MANTIS NAMED SUE
EMERGED FROM AN EGG CASE INTO THE BLUE

BUT ONLY A NYMPH
OUT OF THREE HUNDRED, SHE'S FIFTH.

BABES SEARCHING FOR SCRUMPTIOUS BUG STEW

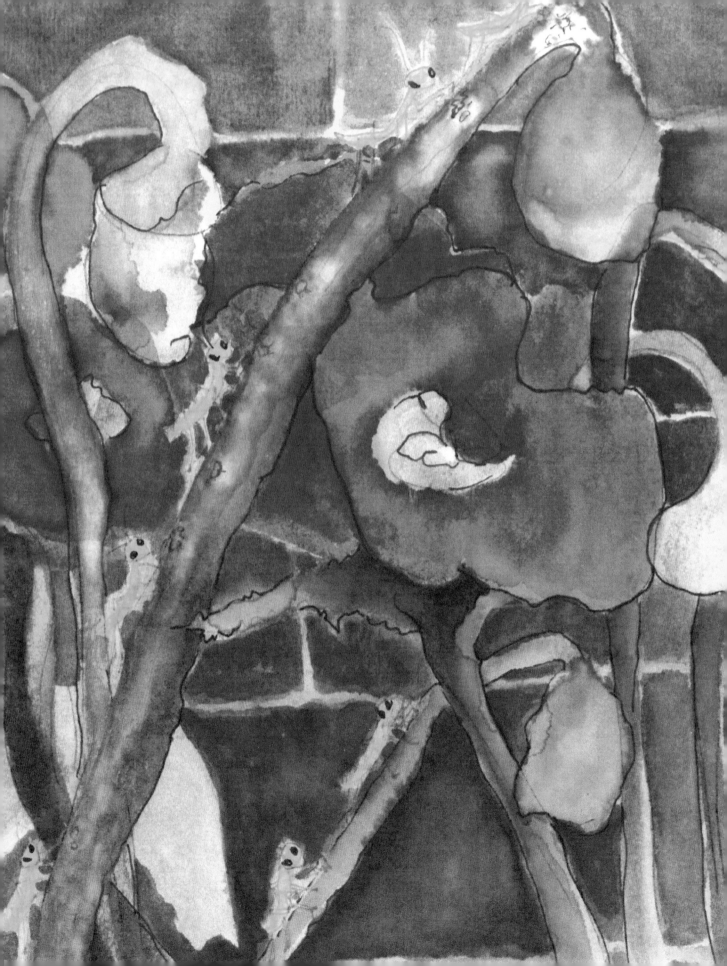

MANTIS NYMPHS MARCH ALONG SINGLE FILE
EATING LEAFHOPPERS AND FLIES ALL THE WHILE

SPIDERS AND APHIDS ARE GREAT
YUMMY MEAT ON THEIR PLATE

KEEPING MANTIDS FULL MILE AFTER MILE

SUE ONCE WAS A NYMPH IN DANGER
OF BECOMING THE MEAL OF A STRANGER

HER SKIN MUST TURN HARD
OR HER FUTURE IS MARRED

BY THE PREDATORS WHO LIVE IN ALL NATURE.

A HUNGRY MANTIS LOOKING FOR A BITE
SOON FINDS HER EXOSKELETON TIGHT

SHE KNOWS SHE MUST SHED
HER SKIN INSTEAD

AND GROW ANOTHER THAT FITS
JUST RIGHT

SUE IS STILL THROUGHOUT THE DAY
ACTING LIKE A TWIG TO LURE HER PREY

TWO SPIKY FRONT CLAWS
ARE QUICK LITTLE PAWS

GRABBING THE INSECTS WHO STRAY

FROM THE BRANCH SUE GOES FLYING
TO A CATERPILLAR SHE IS SPYING

BUT HER THORAX HEARS SOUND
OF A BAT FLYING ROUND

SO SHE HURLS TO THE GROUND DODGING DYING

ON THE GRASS A WAITING MANTIS LIES
CAMOUFLAGE IS SUE'S BEST DISGUISE

HER SKIN IS BROWN GREEN
SO SHE CAN'T BE SEEN

BY INSECTS THAT ARE HALF HER SIZE

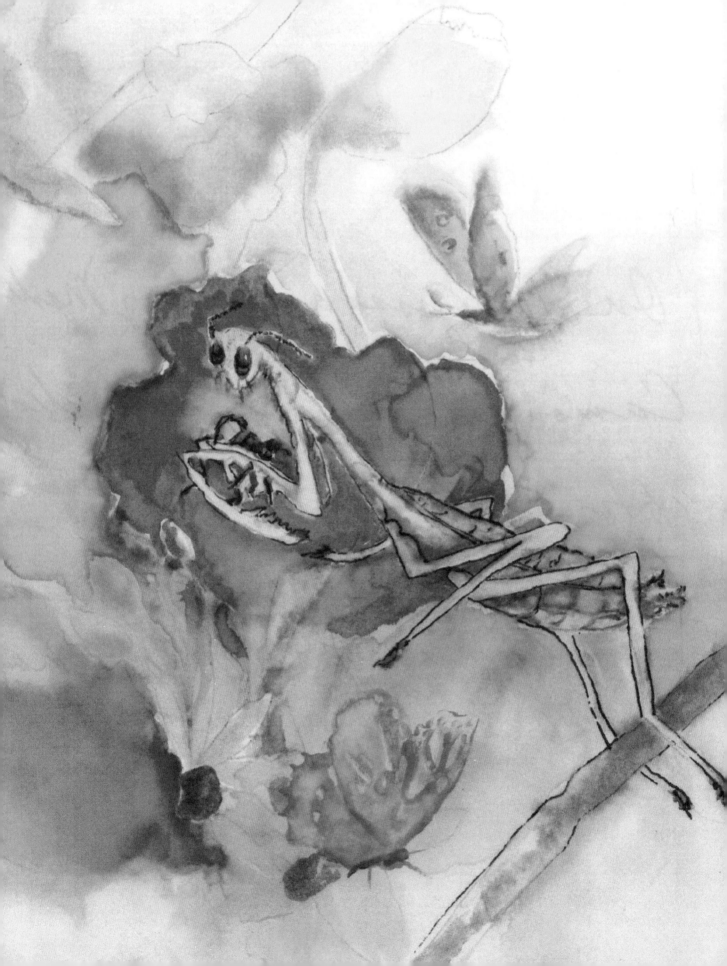

QUIETLY WISHING FOR INSECT STRAYS
SUE PASSES ALONE TIME WHILE SHE PRAYS

WITH EYESIGHT AND STEALTH
SHE RUINS GARDEN PESTS' HEALTH

HUMBLE HUNTING CERTAINLY PAYS

SUE SAW THE REFLECTION IN THE WATER POOL
OF PETER SITTING NEXT TO A GREEN TOADSTOOL

AFTER THAT ONE GLANCE
BEGAN THE DANCE OF ROMANCE

WHICH BETWEEN MANTIDS IS LIFE'S CRUEL RULE

THERE ONCE WAS A MANTIS NAMED PETER
WEDDED SUE ON THE BRANCH OF CEDAR.

THE BABIES THEY MADE
IN AN EGG CASE WERE LAID

BUT A MEAL OF PETER DID FEED HER.

SUE ATTACHED HER EGG CASE TO THE BRUSH
HER FINAL ACT BEFORE ICE SLUSH

WHEN SPRING CAME NEAR
SUE'S BABIES APPEAR

HER LEGACY CONTINUES- WHAT A RUSH!

THE MANTIS HAS SUCH WONDROUS LOOKS
A STICK WITH EYES AND PAWS WITH HOOKS

THEIR HANDSOME MUG
SEEMS SOMETIMES SMUG

ALIEN FEATURES FOUND IN EARTH'S NOOK

THERE ONCE WAS A MANTIS WHO THOUGHT
HE WAS FEARLESS WHENEVER HE FOUGHT

HE WAS A TRUE DRAGON
AND THAT IS NOT BRAGGIN'

FROM HIS MOVES CHINESE KUNG FU IS TAUGHT

THE PRAYING MANTIS BRINGS US CHEER
HIS NAME MEANS PROPHET, A TRUE SEER
HE'LL EAT A BUG
BUT DON'T SAY UGH
OF HIM WE NEED NOT FEAR

SO MANY FACTS WE DO GAIN.
FROM MANTIS RHYMES WHICH ENTERTAIN

OF THIS NOBLE CREATURE
WHO'S THE FEATURE

THERE ARE MORE FACTS TO RETAIN

FUN FACTS

THERE ARE MORE THAN 1800 SPECIES OR VARIETIES OF PRAYING MANTIS.

THE VARIETIES CAME TO THE UNITED STATES AROUND THE 1900'S FROM EUROPE, AFRICA AND CHINA AS GARDEN PREDATORS TO HELP CONTROL GARDEN PESTS.

THE MANTIS IS NAMED FOR ITS PRAYER LIKE STANCE.

THE TWO FORWARD LEGS OF THE MANTIS HAVE SHARP SPINES LIKE A JACKKNIFE.

THE MANTIS FEMALES ARE AMONG THE BIGGEST INSECTS.

THE MANTIS WILL ATTACK BUTTERFLIES, FROGS, SPIDERS, MICE, LIZARDS AND SMALL BIRDS.

SOME SPECIES OF MANTIS ARE THE ONLY INSECTS THAT CAN TURN THEIR HEADS 300 DEGREES AND LOOK OVER THEIR SHOULDERS FOR PREY AND PREDATORS.

THE FEMALE OFTEN EATS THE MALE AFTER MATING.

THE MANTIS HAS VERY GOOD EYESIGHT.

MORE FUN FACTS

MANTIS NYMPHS MARCH SINGLE FILE.

THE NYMPHS HUNT; THEY EAT LEAFHOPPERS, APHIDS AND SMALL FLIES WHICH CAN BE GARDEN PESTS.

THE MANTIS SHEDS ITS SKIN TWELVE TIMES BEFORE IT IS FULLY GROWN.

THE FEMALE MANTIS LAYS HER EGGS IN THE FALL.

THE MANTIS NYMPH IS TINY LIKE A MOSQUITO.

THE FRONT LEGS OF THE NYMPH HAVE CLAWS FOR HOLDING PREY.

THE FEMALE MANTIS CANNOT FLY WHEN SHE HAS MANY EGGS IN HER ABDOMEN.

PRAYING MANTIDS BITE THE BACK OF THEIR VICTIMS' NECK TO PARALYZE IT.

HOW TO CARE FOR MANTIDS

MANTIDS ARE SOME OF THE MOST DIFFICULT OF INSECTS TO REAR. THEY ARE CARNIVORES, THAT IS, THEY EAT SMALLER INSECTS, TINY ANIMALS AND BIRDS. SO THEIR FOOD NEEDS TO BE PROVIDED AND MUST BE GROWN OR GATHERED.

THE TINY NYMPHS TEND TO EAT EACH OTHER, SO THEY NEED TO BE SEPARATED UNTIL GROWN. THE ADULTS WILL THEN MATE IN CAPTIVITY.

THE ADULTS CAN BE FED LARGER INSECTS THAN FLIES, E.G., CRICKETS AND GRASSHOPPERS. (THESE CAN BE PURCHASED IN SOME PET STORES.) IT IS INTERESTING TO WATCH THE MANNER IN WHICH THE MANTIDS ATTACK THE PREY. SOME COLLECTORS LIKE TO WATCH THE FEMALE MANTIDS LAY THEIR EGGS. HOWEVER, MANTIDS USUALLY DIE A FEW WEEKS LATER.

AN EGG CASE THAT IS COLLECTED IN THE FALL MONTHS AND THEN BROUGHT TO A WARM ROOM WILL PROBABLY HATCH IN WINTER OR EARLY SPRING. THE HUNDREDS OF TINY MANTIDS WILL APPEAR; AND IF THEY DO NOT GET FRESH FOOD, THEY WILL EAT EACH OTHER. PERHAPS ONLY ONE OR TWO MANTIDS WILL SURVIVE.

THE PRAYING MANTIS IS VALUABLE AS PART OF A PEST CONTROL PROGRAM. IT IS THE ONLY PREDATOR THAT FEEDS AT NIGHT ON MOTHS. REMEMBER MOTHS ARE ACTIVE ONLY AFTER DARK AND THE MANTIDS ARE FAST ENOUGH TO CATCH THEM AS WELL AS MOSQUITOES AND FLIES.

GLOSSARY

APHID- ANY OF VARIOUS SMALL, SOFT-BODIED INSECTS OF THE FAMILY OF APHIDIDAE THAT HAVE MOUTHPARTS SPECIALLY ADAPTED FOR PIERCING. THEY FEED BY SUCKING SAP FROM OUTDOOR AND INDOOR PLANTS.

CAMOUFLAGE- THE METHOD OR RESULT OF CONCEALING OBJECTS OR PERSONS FROM AN ENEMY BY MAKING THEM APPEAR TO BE PART OF THE NATURAL SURROUNDINGS.

EGG CASE- PROTECTIVE COVERING MADE BY THE FEMALE TO PROTECT HER EGGS

EXOSKELETON- A HARD OUTER STRUCTURE; SUCH AS A SHELL OF AN INSECT OR CRUSTACEAN, THAT PROVIDES PROTECTION OR SUPPORT FOR AN ORGANISM

KUNG FU- ANY OF THE VARIATIONS OF CHINESE MARTIAL ARTS- AN ASIAN FORM OF HAND TO HAND COMBAT.

LEAFHOPPER- ANY OF THE NUMEROUS INSECTS OF THE FAMILY CIRCADELLIDAE THAT SUCK JUICES FROM PLANTS, OFTEN DAMAGING CROPS.

MANTIS- ANY OF THE VARIOUS PREDATORY INSECTS OF THE FAMILY MANTIDAE, PRIMARILY TROPICAL BUT INCLUDING A FEW TEMPERATE ZONE SPECIES, USUALLY PALE GREEN AND HAVING TWO PAIRS OF WALKING LEGS AND POWERFUL GRASPING FORELIMBS. THE MANTIS LIVES ON LIVE INSECTS, INCLUDING OTHERS OF ITS OWN KIND. THEY ARE ALSO CALLED MANTIDS. BOTH TERMS MANTIS AND MANTIDS ARE CORRECT.

GLOSSARY CONTINUED

NYMPH- THE LARVAL FORM OF CERTAIN INSECTS, SUCH AS A GRASSHOPPER, *USUALLY RESEMBLING THE ADULT FORM BUT SMALLER AND LACKING FULLY DEVELOPED WINGS.*

PREDATOR- AN ORGANISM THAT LIVES BY EATING OTHER ORGANISMS.

PROPHET/SEER- A PERSON GIFTED WITH MORAL INSIGHT AND EXCEPTIONAL POWERS OF COMMUNICATION. A PROPHET AND A SEER ARE ALIKE IN THEIR TALENTS. A PROPHET CAN BE CALLED A SEER AND VICE VERSA.

STEALTH- THE ACT OF MOVING, PROCEEDING, OR ACTING IN A COVERT OR SECRET WAY.

SCHEMATIC

A ANTENNAE- TWO LONG ANTENNAE LOCATED ON THE HEAD FOR TOUCH AND SMELL

B COMPOUND EYES- TWO LARGE MULTI-LENSED EYES FOR SIGHT

C HEAD- THE UPPERMOST PART OF THE INSECT, THE EYES, ANTENNAE AND MOUTH ARE ON THE TRIANGULAR SHAPED HEAD

D MANDIBLES- THE JAWS ARE USED TO CHEW FOOD,

E THORAX- THE MIDDLE PART OF THE INSECT BODY. THE LEGS AND WINGS ARE ATTACHED TO THE THORAX. THE FIRST SEGMENT IS THE PROTHORAX.

F FRONT LEGS- GRASPING TWO FRONT LEGS TO CATCH AND HOLD PREY

G WINGS- TWO PAIRS OF WINGS(4) ATTACHED TO THE THORAX

H WALKING LEGS- TWO PAIRS OF LEGS USED FOR CLIMBING, WALKING AND JUMPING

I ABDOMEN- THE SEGMENT THAT CONTAINS THE DIGESTIVE TRACT AND REPRODUCTIVE ORGANS

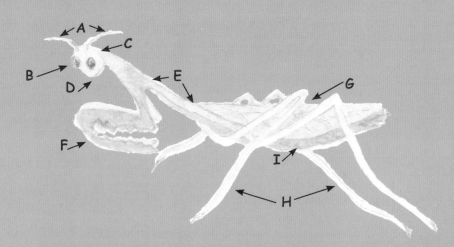

MANTIDS OF THE WORLD

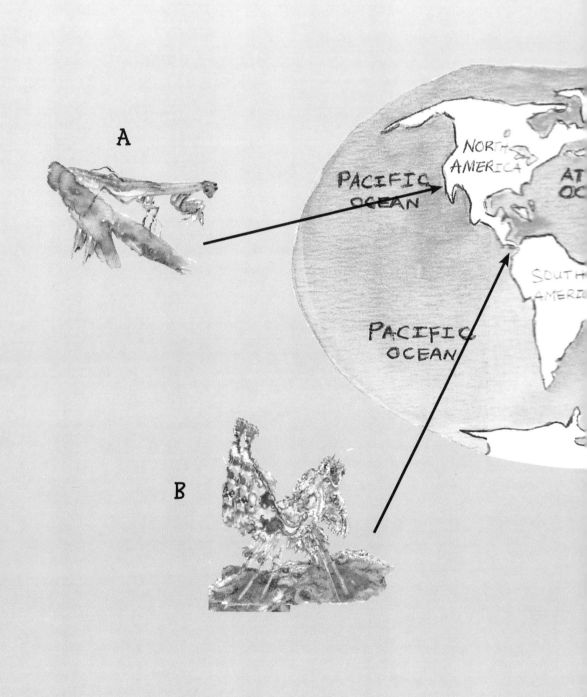

A CAROLINA MANTID
B ECUADORIAN MANTID

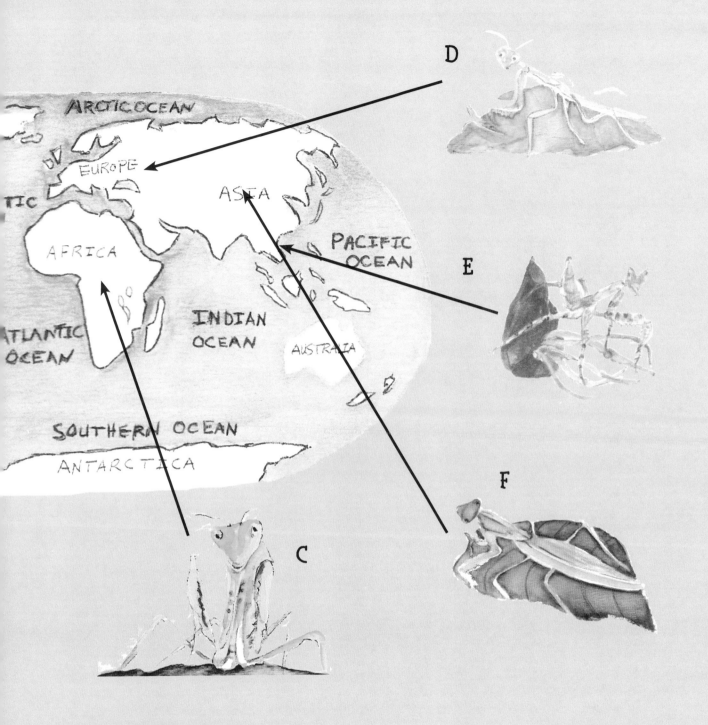

C AFRICAN MANTID
D EUROPEAN MANTID
E BURMESE FLOWER MANTID
F CHINESE MANTID

PRAYING MANTIS HABITAT OR MANTIDS OF THE WORLD

THERE ARE APPROXIMATELY 1800 OR MORE DIFFERENT SPECIES OF MANTIDS. ALL OF THEM ARE INSECTS WITH SIX LEGS. EACH SPECIES HAS SPECIAL TRAITS WITHIN THE MANTIS FAMILY. MOST ARE TROPICAL OR SUBTROPICAL, BUT SEVERAL SPECIES LIVE IN TEMPERATE CLIMATES LIKE THE UNITED STATES AND CENTRAL EUROPE. SPECIES WERE BROUGHT TO THE UNITED STATES AROUND THE 1900'S FROM EUROPE AND CHINA AS GARDEN PREDATORS TO CONTROL PESTS.

THE **CAROLINA MANTIS** WILL AVERAGE 4-7 CENTIMETERS BUT CAN GROW TO 10 CENTIMETERS. THE BODY IS YELLOWISH-BROWN WITH THE WING MARGINS IN A PEA GREEN COLOR. THE FRONT LEGS ARE MODIFIED TO ACT LIKE A POCKET KNIFE TO HOLD THEIR PREY.

THE **ECUADORIAN MANTIS** HAS THE ABILITY TO ADAPT TO ITS SURROUNDNGS. THE MANTID GROWS 1.2 CM TO 13 CM AND USES COLORATION, STRUCTURAL CHANGES AND BEHAVIORS TO CATCH PREY.

THE **AFRICAN MANTIS** WILL GROW 7-10 CENTIMETERS. COLORS WILL RANGE FROM DARK BROWN TO BRIGHT GREEN. ADULTS ARE

FULLY WINGED AND WILL OFTEN RESEMBLE FLOWERS SO CLOSELY THAT INSECTS WILL OFTEN LAND ON THEM FOR NECTAR.

THE **EUROPEAN MANTIS** IS THE STATE INSECT OF CONNECTICUT, BUT ORIGINATED IN NORTHERN AFRICA, SOUTHERN EUROPE AND ASIA. THEY AVERAGE 5-6 CENTIMETERS IN LENGTH AND ARE USUALLY GREEN OR BROWN.

THE **BURMESE FLOWER MANTIS** CAN MIMIC THE TEXTURE AND COLOR OF ITS SURROUNDINGS. THE MANTID CAN MIMIC PLANT STAMENS, TWIGS, STONES AND ANTS TO HUNT PREY AND HIDE FROM PREDATORS. BURMA IS NOW CALLED MYANMAR.

THE **CHINESE MANTIS** IS LONG AND THIN WITH COLORS RANGING IN DIFFERENT SHADES OF BROWN. WHEN ADULT, THEY HAVE A GREEN STRIPE DOWN THE SIDE OF THE WING CASE. THE ADULT VARIES FROM 8-10 CENTIMETERS IN LENGTH.

MANTIS JUMBLE

WHAT DID SUE, THE PRAYING MANTIS, DO WHEN SHE WAS HUNGRY?

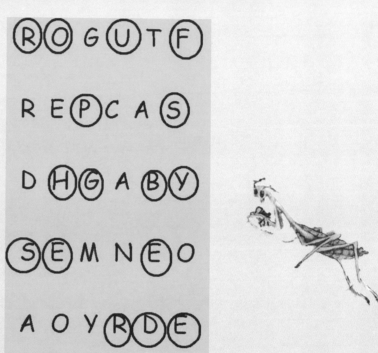

R O G U T F

R E P C A S

D H G A B Y

S E M N E O

A O Y R D E

TAKE ALL OF THE CIRCLED LETTERS,

UNSCRAMBLE TO FILL IN THE BLANKS.

_ _ _ _ _ _ _ _ _ _ _ _ _ _ _ _ _

THE ANSWER TO THE QUESTION WHAT DID SUE DO WHEN SHE WAS HUNGRY?

_ _ _ _ _ _ _ _

_ _ _ _ _ _ _ .

MANTIS WORD FIND

PREYING, PETER, SUE, THORAX, ANTENNAE, KUNG FU
EGG SAC, FORELEGS, BUG, MANTID

LOOK VERTICALLY, HORIZONTALLY, FORWARD, BACKWARD AND DIAGONALLY

F	O	R	E	L	E	G	S	R	Z
P	R	E	Y	I	N	G	A	E	L
G	M	B	U	G	S	D	N	J	E
D	J	R	P	P	E	T	E	R	G
I	B	N	M	C	N	S	T	A	G
T	S	U	O	S	U	E	E	S	S
N	T	H	O	R	A	X	T	C	A
A	A	N	T	E	N	N	A	E	C
M	O	Y	K	U	N	G	F	U	T
W	I	N	G	K	E	S	O	S	S

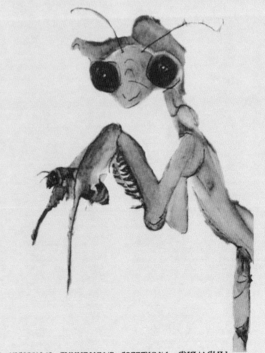

BONUS QUESTIONS
1. HAS CLAWS

_ _ _ _ _ _ _ _

2. FOUND ON THE HEAD

_ _ _ _ _ _ _ _

3. PICKS UP SOUNDS

_ _ _ _ _ _

4. HUNTING

_ _ _ _ _ _

5. HAS 300 EGGS

_ _ _ _ _ _ _

MAKE YOUR OWN PRAYING MANTIS FINGER PUPPET

READ ALL THE DIRECTIONS FIRST

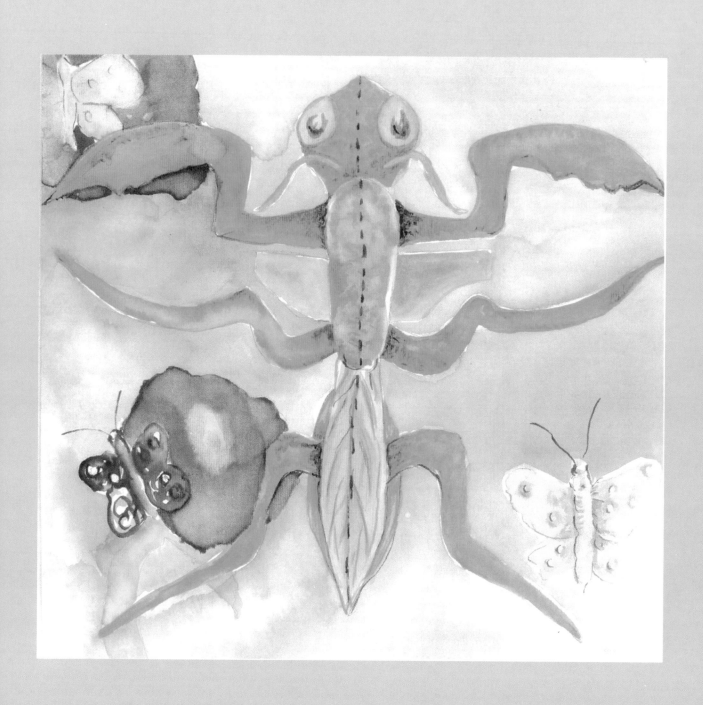

1. TRACE THE MANTIS ON ANOTHER SHEET OF PAPER OR CAREFULLY REMOVE THIS PAGE.

2. FOLD THE PAGE IN HALF ALONG THE MIDDLE OF THE MANTIS.

3. CUT OUT THE MANTIS.

4. FOLD THE FINGER TABS TOGETHER AND TAPE THEM TO FIT YOUR FINGER.

NOW READ <u>PERPETUALLY PREYING PRAYING MANTIS</u>
WITH YOUR OWN FINGER PUPPET

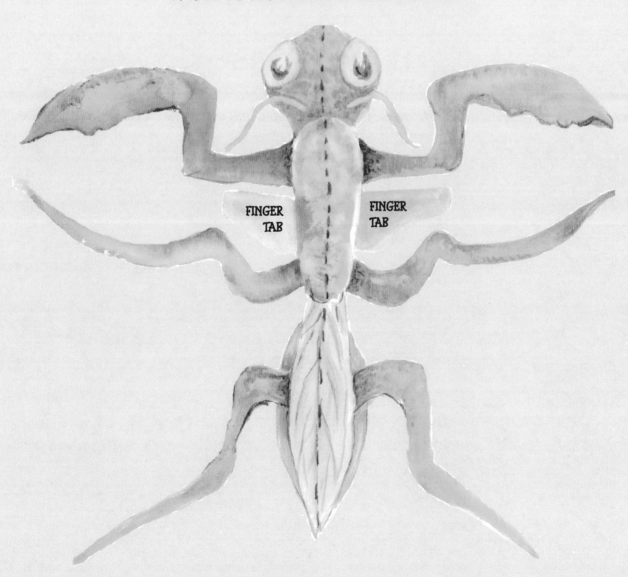

FINGER TAB

FINGER TAB